200 Tricky Spellings
in Cartoons

200 Tricky Spellings in Cartoons

Visual Mnemonics for Everyone

Lidia Stanton

Illustrated by Sophie Kennedy

Jessica Kingsley Publishers
London and Philadelphia

First published in Great Britain in 2021 by Jessica Kingsley Publishers
An Hachette Company

1

Front cover image source: Sophie Kennedy.

The fonts, layout and overall design of this book have been prepared according to dyslexia-friendly principles. At JKP we aim to make our books' content accessible to as many readers as possible.

A CIP catalogue record for this title is available from the British Library and the Library of Congress

ISBN 978 1 78775 540 6
eISBN 978 1 78775 541 3

Printed and bound in the United States by Integrated Books International

Jessica Kingsley Publishers' policy is to use papers that are natural, renewable and recyclable products and made from wood grown in sustainable forests. The logging and manufacturing processes are expected to conform to the environmental regulations of the country of origin.

Jessica Kingsley Publishers
Carmelite House
50 Victoria Embankment
London EC4Y 0DZ

www.jkp.com

Contents

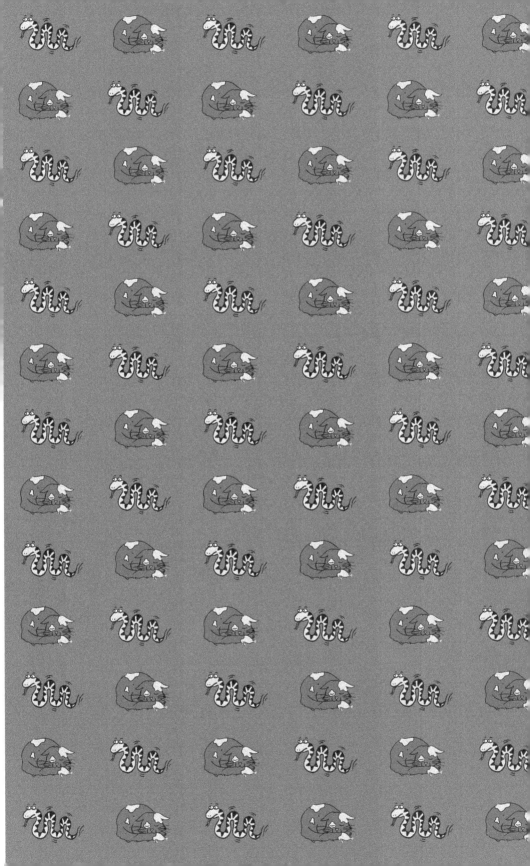

1

What Are Mnemonics?

The word "mnemonic" is pronounced with a silent front letter m [ni'monic].

Mnemonics are memory triggers that help us remember things we easily forget, for example tricky spellings. We can readily recall mnemonics because of their funny and unusual associations with things that are part of our daily lives. Best of all, mnemonics require almost no effort to learn.

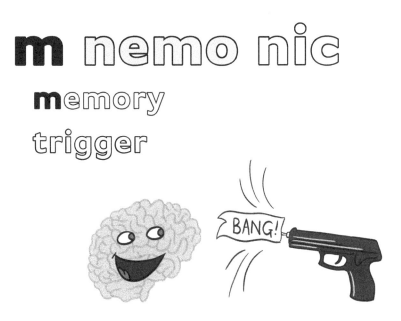

m nemo nic
memory
trigger

But how to remember the spelling of "mnemonic"? We can make the front letter "m" stand for "memory," or better still "memory trigger." **M**nemonics trigger our **m**emory.

There is also the tricky-to-spell "nemo" part. What's that? Nemo is a lovable orange and white fish? Perfect. Now think of his blue friend with amnesia. Dory's constant forgetfulness makes her all the more unforgettable to us. We laugh and cry with her, and with Nemo.

Think *mnemonic*, think *memory trigger* and *Nemo*.

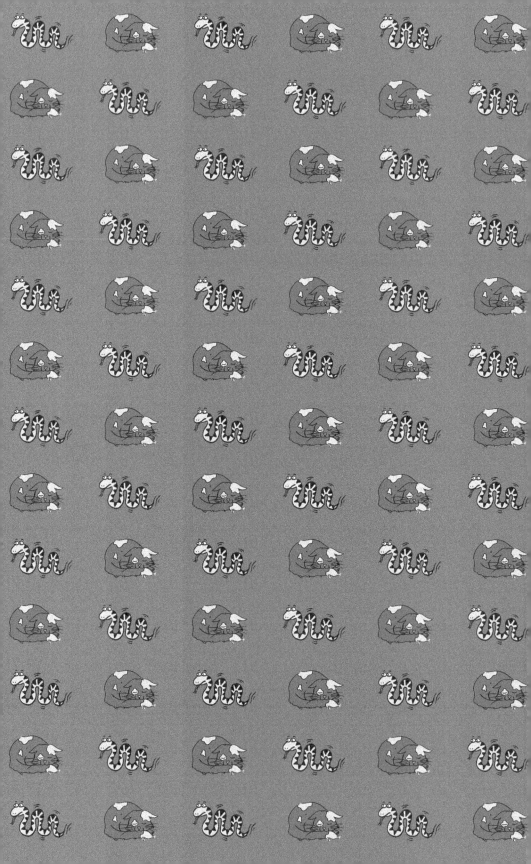

2

How to Use This Book

Look up the word that you find difficult to spell in the book's index. Each chapter lists words alphabetically.

Reference books like this one don't need to be read from cover to cover.

Enjoy the cartoons with visual hints and story lines. They are designed to be funny, silly, bold and occasionally wicked (a bra is mentioned a good few times).

Okay, some story lines are plain crazy to make them more memorable. If you want to learn to spell in a fun, intelligent and virtually effortless way, open up your mind and let your imagination run loose.

Think of the story behind each spelling mnemonic. Make sure you understand the connection. Don't be discouraged if some hints make more sense than others.

Own the story—modify it so that it makes full sense to you. Think of your past experiences and link the spelling to your own life stories.

Use the newly learned mnemonic the same day. We tend to forget most of what we learn within the first 24 hours.

The best way to learn is to teach. Share the spelling hint with other people, in person or online. Tell them why it works for you. Show it off in the classroom or in the office, or use it as a party trick.

Be practical. Create posters and other artwork with the spelling hints and display them around your home to remind you what you've learned. Make the artwork as fun and colorful as possible.

Turn the cartoons in this book into coloring pages. They've been left black and white so you can use highlighters and markers to make your learning active and fun. Be creative. Own the cartoons.

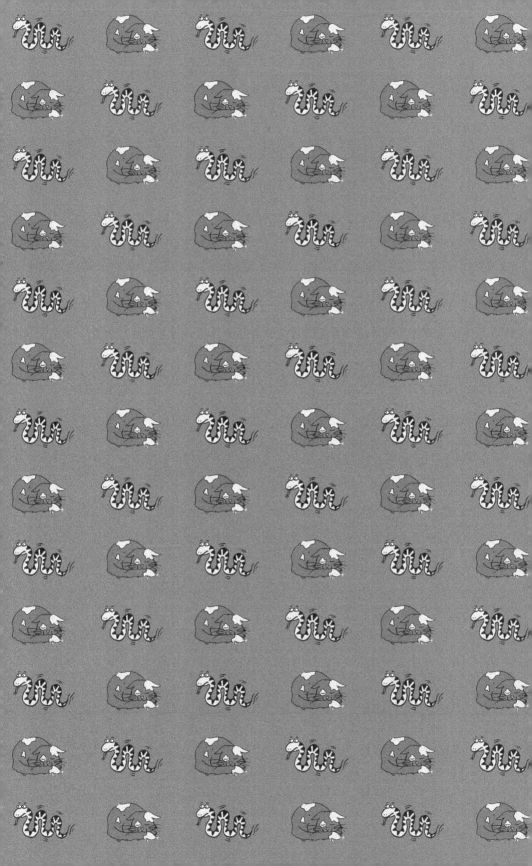

3

Confusing Pairs
of Words

These are words that sound the same but are spelled differently (homophones),

or

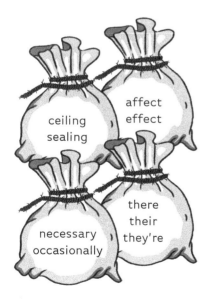

words that somehow "go together"—either because they belong to the same word category, or because they have similar meaning, pronunciation, or spelling patterns.

ACCEPT vs. EXCEPT

ACCEPT

accept
accept a call

Accept **a c**all,

EXCEPT

except
in exams

except in **ex**ams!

No **except**ions, **X**ander. Make your way to the **ex**it.

ADAPT vs. ADOPT

ADAPT

All living things have evolved to ad**a**pt to ch**a**nge. Every day we ad**a**pt to fit in.

It fascinates me how Adam's green sweatsuit is the exact color of the shrubs behind the running track. In fact, I'm struggling to spot him right now. I don't think he likes sports very much...

ADOPT

When you ad**o**pt a pet, you **o**wn them and they **o**wn you, for life.

Ask an ad**o**ptive family if they remember a time when their pet didn't live with them.

AFFECT vs. EFFECT

AFFECT

Suri's stunning looks **a**ffected Adam's **a**bility to see where he was going.

EFFECT

The **e**ffect was less stunning.
One person's **a**ction (Suri applied a new lipstick that day) **a**ffected the behavior of the other.

And the r**e**sult, or **e**ffect?
Adam is love-struck. Or is that a "wall-struck" **e**ffect?

AISLE vs. ISLE

AISLE

Aisle **A is le**gendary for its **a**ccidents. Last week's **a**wkward **a**nnouncements included:

"**A**ntibacterial clean-up in **A**isle **A**.
Abandoned **a**vocados."

"**A**ttempted **a**lien **a**bduction. **A**void **A**isle **A**."

"**A**ggravated **a**nimal **a**pprehended in **A**isle **A**."

"**A**dvertising **a**ssistant **a**sleep in **A**isle **A**.
Manager **a**ware."

ISLE

An **isl**e **is l**and.

Did you know there is an actual isle of dogs in the U.K.? The geographical location of London's financial center in Canary Wharf with its tallest and most impressive skyscrapers is the **Isle of Dogs**. Before London became industrialized, it used to be a quiet island, mostly rural, and it is believed to have been home to stray dogs.

ASSURE vs. REASSURE

ASSURE

Adam **as**sured Mr. and Mrs. Pleasant that he was the best neighbor they could wish for: "Rest **as**sured I'm not into partying. **Sure** as a pickle."

When you **as**sure someone, you tell them with confidence that something will or will not happen, and they usually believe you.

REASSURE

Sadly, Adam only put his neighbors' minds to rest, not their ears! Now he has to **reas**sure them he *can* be trustworthy.

When you **reas**sure someone, you make their worry go away by making them feel better, or feel relieved.

BEAR vs. BARE

BEAR

How can b**ear**s be both cute and big and scary? Because of their tiny **ear**s.

In fact, polar b**ear**s have small **ear**s to avoid losing heat. This way, they can stay warm in very cold climates.

BARE

"What **are** you doing, standing by the **bar** completely **bar**e? I can **bar**ely look at you."
"What do you mean? I'm wearing a **ba**ndana on my head."
"Quick! Run before the **bar**tender will see you!"

BORED vs. BOARD

BORED

Mom says she is bo**red** of **red** dresses, shoes and lipsticks.

Dad never gets bo**red** of the color **red** on Mom. He is only bo**red** when waiting at a **red** light.

"The average American spends 3520 minutes, or 58.6 hours, waiting at **red** lights. Put another way: that's 122 days, or about 4 months of your life," he reads in a magazine.

BOARD

card
board

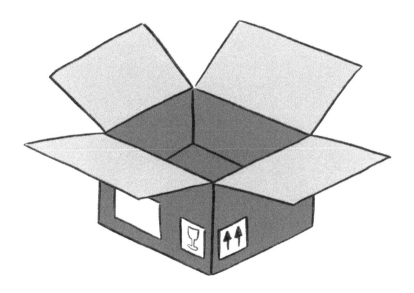

Virtually all cardbo**ard** boxes are made of c**ard**.

That's the spelling of "bo**ard**" sorted.

BRAKE vs. BREAK

BRAKE

Bradley had to **bra**ke so hard that he scraped asphalt off the road to avoid driving into a **bra**.

He learned the spelling of the word "**bra**ke" for life.

BREAK

break
heart

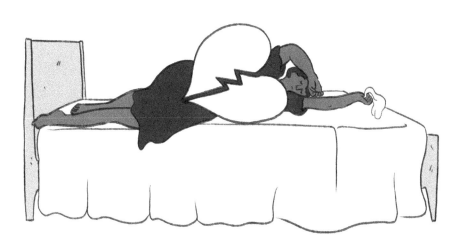

Don't br**ea**k anybody's h**ea**rt—they only have one.

CEILING vs. SEALING

CEILING

ceiling
every
inch
ceiling
certfied

"**E**very **i**nch of our **cei**ling is **ce**rtified. A **ce**rtified **cei**ling won't **c**rack or **c**ollapse," announced **Ce**drick watching his co-worker close the property's door as slowly and as gently as he could.

Phew... That was **c**lose.

SEALING

sealing

To **sea**l all cracks in the stairs, **Sea**n needed a bucket load of trade glue. One might say, it was a **sea** of **sea**lants.

CHILI vs. CHILLY vs. CHILE

CHILI

Cheeseburgers with onions and tomatoes? Not for Dad. He likes to put a whole hot ch**ili** in them.

Look at the spelling pattern of ch**ili**. The "l" is squeezed between two letter "i"s, just like Dad's chili is squished between two soft buns.

The hottest chili Dad has ever tried was called Dragon's Breath. He didn't speak for five days. Not that he had to—Mom did all the complaining for him.

CHILLY

I love my chill**y** walks
in special thermal socks.
When they get crisp and ic**y**,
my feet are warming nice**ly**.
Why are my feet not ic**y**?
The thermal socks were price**y**.

CHILE

Chile

ends of the earth

Historians speculate that the name Chil**e** might originate from an Indigenous word for "**e**nds of the **e**arth," or "where the land **e**nds."

Chil**e** is the longest and narrowest country in the world, which explains the "**e**nds" rather than "**e**nd" of the earth. It stretches from the north to the south over 2670 miles (4300 kilometers).

Notes

COLLEGE vs. COLLAGE

COLLEGE

A college is a place of education.

How was Pasadena City College described in the TV series *The Big Bang Theory*?

Oh, yes. A place for fun and a place for knowledge. Leonard has a real way with words...

COLLAGE

A collage is the art of putting together pieces of different materials, such as pictures, photographs and fabrics, on one surface to create an image.

An artist assembles a collage.

A buyer beholds it, and a critic comments on it.

COMMITTEE vs. COMMISSION

COMMITTEE

The animals went in **two by two**. Hoorah! Hoorah!

That's why Noah's ark's co**mm**i**tt**ee consisted of **two m**onkeys, **two t**igers and **two e**lephants.

COMMISSION

There was also a special co**mm**i**ss**ion, where the **two** **m**onkeys were joined by **two s**nakes.

With this much executive control, Noah's powers to keep dinosaurs, griffins and unicorns on board were seriously limited.

COMPLEMENT vs. COMPLIMENT

COMPLEMENT

complement
complete

Butter completes bread—the two complement each other.

Other matching pairs are hamburgers and fries, salt and pepper, pen and paper, Tom and Jerry, Mario and Luigi, Bert and Ernie, Mulder and Scully, Sherlock and that doctor... Doctor Who or Dr. Watson?

COMPLIMENT

compliment
i like

Who doesn't like compliments?

"**I** like nothing more than a genuine, heart-felt compliment," said Ken while studying himself in a mirror.

Barbie's face lit up. She looked up and whispered: "Go ahead. **I**'m ready for the compliment!"

DESERT vs. DESSERT

DESERT

Fewer than a quarter of all known de**s**erts are covered in **s**and, yet when we hear the word "de**s**ert," we think of **s**and.

Icy Antarctica is the largest cold de**s**ert on Earth. It's bigger than the **S**ahara with all its **s**and spreading over 11 countries!

DESSERT

The word "de**ss**ert" comes from the French "de**ss**ervir," which means "to clear the table."

I know someone who holds an unofficial world record for fastest table clearing when **s**weet **s**tuff is served!

EMIGRATE vs. IMMIGRATE

EMIGRATE

When you **e**migrate, you **e**xit (leave) your country to live in another one.

When goods are sold to another country, it's called **e**xport, as they **e**xit (leave) the country.

IMMIGRATE

immigrate
into

When you **i**mmigrate, you come **i**nto a new country.

When goods are bought from another country, it's called **i**mport, as they come **i**nto the country.

ENSURE vs. INSURE

ENSURE

To **en**sure complete s**e**curity of his apartment, Enrique would lock the door and then try different ways of forcing it open before leaving for work in the morning.

Only then did he hear a little voice in his head say: "Well done, Enrique. Now you've really made c**e**rtain your model train collection is safe."

INSURE

insure
injury

Jim only learned the real value of his car **in**surance after he drove into a black limousine with a plate "**In**sured by Mafia. You hit us, we hit you."

From then on, when Jim thought of **in**surance, he immediately thought of **in**jury.

FLOUR vs. FLOWER

FLOUR

Mom only uses fl**our** from **our** local mill because it makes the best bread, cake and pancakes.

She calls, "Get me f**our** pounds of **our** fl**our**!" and one of us runs to the local mill.

FLOWER

Why do we love fl**ower**s? Their beauty feeds our souls. Their colors and smells seduce us so that we give them full attention. That is their secret p**ower**—fl**ower** p**ower**.

I find it a nice, nostalgic thought that in the 60s and 70s people believed that fl**ower** p**ower** would make the world a better, safer place.

HAIR vs. HARE

HAIR

I dry my h**air** in the **air**.

Unless it's humid out there—I don't want to be a Lion King.

HARE

hare

Apparently, you **are** faster than Tortoise, H**are**.

Are you?

HOLE vs. WHOLE

HOLE

A ring doughnut has a **hole**.

WHOLE

A jam doughnut doesn't.
What happened to the **hole**?
It's now inside the w**hole** doughnut.

"hole" is inside "whole"

LOSE vs. LOOSE

LOSE

It's easy to l**o**se track of how fast we l**o**se m**o**ney because each time we tend to think of it as a **single** amount:

"I didn't l**o**se one hundred dollars; I spent a **single** amount that was $100."

LOOSE

Why does Betty have l**oo**se teeth?

She's English and she says "candy floss" instead of "cotton candy." Betty thought candy floss and dental floss were the same thing!

But there is something that keeps her loose teeth together. It's t**oo**thpaste.

MADE vs. MAID

MADE

We've all ma**de** bad **de**cisions at some point.

This morning I ma**de** my bed. Now my cat has moved out.

MAID

Since ma**id**s became known as housekeepers and house cleaners, they wear **ID** pins on their uniforms.

Take V.A. Cuuming, L. Aundry, I. Roning and C. Lean— all very professional staff with impressive badges.

NECESSARY vs. OCCASIONALLY

NECESSARY

It is ne**cess**ary for Mom to have **c**offee with **two s**ugars.

One coffee, **two s**ugars.

One C, two Ss.

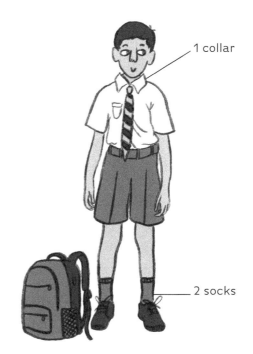

1 collar

2 socks

Dad prefers to draw a schoolboy with **one c**ollar and **two s**ocks.

One C, two Ss.

OCCASIONALLY

Occasionally, Mom makes **two c**offees (one for her, one for Aunt Ruth) with only **one s**poonful of sugar split between the two cups.

Two coffees, one sugar.

Two Cs, one S.

Dad draws a boy with **two c**ollars and **one s**ock.

Two Cs, one S.

He explains: "The boy was in a hurry to kick the ball after school and didn't take his shirt off—he's wearing two collars. He didn't care he'd lost a sock and rushed onto the field."

2 collars

1 sock

PEACE vs. PIECE

PEACE

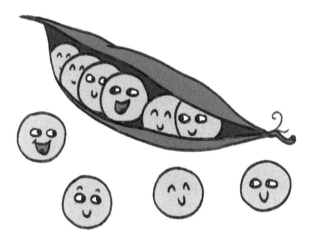

A tiny **pea** is a very **pea**ceful creature. It's so **pea**ceful that Green**pea**ce used its color to represent their values.

Green **pea** = green **pea**ce = Green**pea**ce

Really? Hang on a minute. Peter has made it all up. But what a story...

Now you remember the spelling of "**pea**ce."

PIECE

There's nothing else to say other than: "Have a **pie**ce of **pie**."

PERSUADE vs. PURSUE

PERSUADE

I've been trying to **per**suade **Ade** to learn to cook before serving dinner. It looks like my efforts have paid off. No revolting dinner tonight (thank goodness!), though I'm not sure why I have to pack my bags.

When you **per**suade someone, you convince them to think or do something. You **per**suade a **per**son.

PURSUE

pursue
you run after

The police pu**r**sued **Sue**'s car with helicopters. She was pur**sue**d because she had broken the law: "Did you, or did you not, post pictures of your neighbor's cat as your own, **Sue**?"

When you pu**rsue** someone or something, yo**u r**un after them (follow them) trying to catch them.

The two letters "**u**" in "p**u**rs**u**e" are there to remind you that anyone who wants to get to you (**2 u**) is p**u**rs**u**ing you.

PHYSIOLOGY vs. PSYCHOLOGY

PHYSIOLOGY

physiology
peppermint
helps
your
stomach

Physiology is about normal functioning of living organisms and their parts, such as the digestive system. There are many natural remedies that stimulate physiological processes in humans and animals. For example, peppermint helps relax the digestive system and even ease stomach pain.

PSYCHOLOGY

Freud argued that it was your mom who single-handedly "spoiled you, child." Modern psychology came to recognize that it's only fair that both parents share the blame.

Both **psych**ology and **psych**iatry have the same prefix "**psych**." Is there any difference between the two?

Psychiatrists are medically trained, **psych**ologists are not.

PRECEDENT vs. PRESIDENT

PRECEDENT

A pre**ce**dent is a **pre**vious **c**ase or **e**xample that has become a reference for new decisions.

By allowing [**AQ**]**Ce**cil to watch a late night movie, Dad has established a pre**ce**dent for the future. He can now expect **Ce**cil to yell "But you let me stay up before!" tomorrow, the day after tomorrow, and every night until **Ce**cil is 18 years old.

PRESIDENT

president
sometimes
impeached

Franklin Delano Roosevelt said that presidents are selected, not elected.

"And **s**ometimes **i**mpeached!" Dad had to put his two cents in.

In the U.S., a president may be impeached (challenged or called into question because of their integrity) for treason, bribery, or high crimes and misdemeanors.

PRINCIPAL vs. PRINCIPLE

PRINCIPAL

A fortune cookie told Jaime that the first person he would greet in the morning was his best **pal** for life.

The Princi**pal** was not impressed.
Poor Jaime.
Detention for a week.

PRINCIPLE

It's always best to follow rules as a matter of princi**ple**, but what about rules that have a double meaning?

Here's one:

SLOW
MEN AT WORK

"**Ple**ase Slow Down" would do just the trick.

PRONOUNCE vs. PRONUNCIATION

PRONOUNCE

We gave it every **ounce** of effort to correctly pron**ounce** Celtic names we were not familiar with.

It's always best to ask the person how they say their name, then think of a mnemonic that will help us remember it. Every time I see Seamus in college, I think, "What a shame I can't pron**ounc**e names better."

PRONUNCIATION

pronunCIAtion

Sister Louisa was a most trustworthy and dependable **nun**.

Once, the **CIA** tried to make her confess correct pro**nuncia**tion of secret words.

Worry not. **Nun**'s the word.

QUIET vs. QUITE

QUIET

It was quiet **in** **e**very **t**own when al**ie**ns were meant to arrive. People were told to give them some space.

QUITE

Frank only sometimes opens doors for other people. But he always lets his dog pass through first.

Frank isn't terribly pol**ite**. He is only qu**ite** pol**ite**.

SIGHT vs. SITE vs. CITE

SIGHT

Anyone can have perfect si**gh**t. Just pop your **g**lasses on!

Glasses **h**elp with your si**gh**t.

Now that's a si**gh** of relief...

SITE

site
setting
location

You are allowed to **sit** down on **sit**e, especially a camp or picnic **sit**e, though not building **sit**es.

Web**sit**es are tricky, unless they're baby-**sit**ting or house-**sit**ting web**sit**es.

CITE

cite
citation

When **c**iting (quoting) word for word, be sure to avoid **c**opyright **c**overed works. These can be words taken from books, films, computer games, advertisements and lots of other protected sources. Breaking **c**opyright laws is called plagiarism.

To avoid plagiarism, always **c**ite your sources.

Think *cite*, think *copyright*.

Notes

SPECIFIC vs. PACIFIC

SPECIFIC

When something is **spe**cific, it's particular rather than general. It's **spe**cially **s**et so it's clear what it is. It's better to have *specific* instructions than general ones.

A **spe**cific question is not any question. It's the one we are focusing on now.

A **spe**cific task is not any task. It's the one set by the teacher five minutes ago.

Would you say I've been quite **spe**cific about what *specific* means?

PACIFIC

Pacific
paddling

How big of a **pa**ddle do I need to k**a**yak **a**cross the **Pa**cific Ocean?

A **pa**ddle?! You are joking, **Pa**t! Unless you're thinking of a **p**ond. The **Pa**cific Ocean is *the* biggest ocean on Earth. Go figure.

STATIONARY vs. STATIONERY

STATIONARY

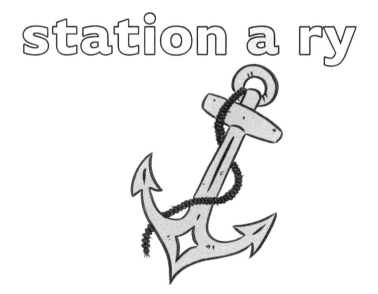

Ahoy, Matey. Ye want t'be station**a**ry?

Anchor the ship then, **ar**rr.

STATIONERY

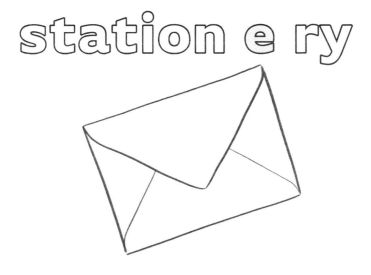

We asked 100 people to name an item of station**e**ry.

Ninety-nine said "**e**nvelope."

STEEL vs. STEAL

STEEL

What does st**ee**l f**ee**l like?
Cold and hard, and if it's a transmission tower,
like danger.

STEAL

steal
dream

"If you had to, would you ever st**ea**l?"

"I'd st**ea**l a dr**ea**m, but nothing r**ea**l, like a m**ea**l."

"A fair d**ea**l."

THAN vs. THEN

THAN

Ju-Long was taller than Luis.
Why did Luis borrow a ladder before he went to see
Ju-Long?

So they could see eye to eye.

THEN

"And then I... I..."

"What *did* you do n**e**xt?"

"Th**e**n I apologized."

"Oh, that's settled th**e**n."

THEIR vs. THERE vs. THEY'RE

THEIR

For the th**ir**d time this week, the g**ir**ls got d**ir**t in the**ir** ha**ir** and on the**ir** sh**ir**ts and sk**ir**ts. Ask them to wash and **ir**on the**ir** uniforms, or the**ir** teacher will grow t**ir**ed of the**ir** antics.

THERE

"T**here** they are." "W**here**?"

Start with **HERE**. If it's not **HERE**, it's over T**HERE**.

W**HERE**?

Over T**HERE**.

THEY'RE

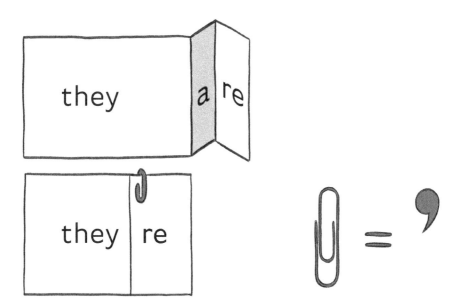

Think *paper clip*, think *apostrophe*.

Notes

TOO vs. TWO

TOO

T**oo**n was t**oo** c**oo**l for sch**oo**l.

But homeschooling bored him t**oo**.

Is T**oo**n t**oo** c**oo**l to learn?
T**oo** clever for his own g**oo**d?

TWO

There can only be **tw**o **tw**ins.

One, two.
Two **tw**irling and **tw**isting **tw**ins.

WASTE vs. WAIST

WASTE

waste
step back!

Step back **Ste**fan!
There is no more room for all the wa**ste** on our planet.

WAIST

"I do have a small waist!" protested Ian before holding his breath in for so long that he became an hourglass.

WEAR vs. WHERE

WEAR

Earrings were originally **ring**s that women attached to their **ear** lobes (**ear rings**). Nowadays, we have all sorts of pierced and non-pierced (clip on) **ear**rings that both women and men can w**ear**.

WHERE

"T**here** they are." "W**here**?"

Start with **HERE**. If it's not **HERE**, it's over T**HERE**.

WHERE?

Over T**HERE**.

WEATHER vs. WHETHER

WEATHER

What's the w**ea**ther at **sea** like today?

The w**ea**ther at **sea** is not looking great.

A storm is on its way.

WHETHER

He thought long and hard about w**he**ther **he** should do it.

"I don't know w**he**ther I should apply for the job, or w**he**ther I should stay in school," he said.

He didn't realize it then but only **he** knew the answer.

WHO'S vs. WHOSE

WHO'S

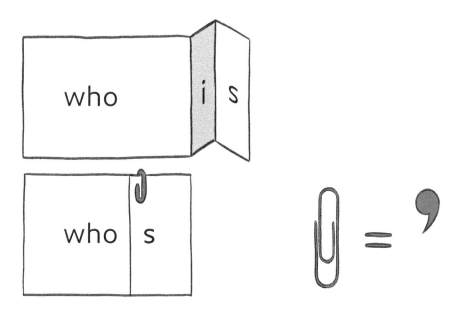

Think *paper clip*, think *apostrophe*.

WHOSE

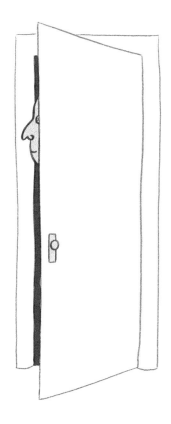

Wh**ose** n**ose** is that?

Someone is being very n**ose**y.

WITCH vs. WHICH

WITCH

Why do **wit**ches cackle?

Because they are **wit**ty.

But why do w**itch**es ride on broomsticks?

Because they have **itch**y feet.

WHICH

which

wh ?

who
what
where
when
why

Which is yet another question that starts with "**wh.**"

YOUR vs. YOU'RE

YOUR

Checklist:

- Does it belong to him, her or them?
- Do they own it?

If you answered YES:
Put the "**r**" at the end of "you**r**." Just as the trademark sign ® is placed after a name that is protected because it belongs to an organization.

If you answered NO:
It's "you're." No "r" at the end of the word.

YOU'RE

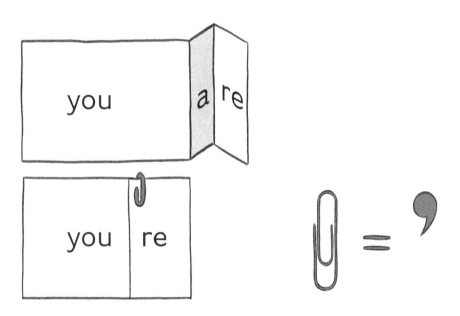

Think *paper clip*, think *apostrophe*.

S or C?

ADVI**S**E vs. ADVI**C**E
DEVI**S**E vs. DEVI**C**E

Meet **S**nake, an active animal that **s**lides in a
serpentine motion.

Cat, on the other hand, is a **c**omfort **c**reature that
lacks any motivation to be active when it doesn't have
to be.

These two have important jobs to do when it comes to the spelling of:

ADVI**S**E vs. ADVI**C**E
DEVI**S**E vs. DEVI**C**E

doing word

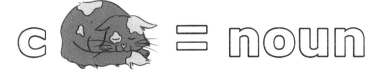

non-doing word

When you advi**s**e someone, you do it actively by speaking or writing to them. In contrast, a pie**c**e of advi**c**e, or the advi**c**e, is given to you without any effort on your part.

The **s**truggle to devi**s**e a phone without a wire was real. Now that we have the devi**ce**, it's called a **ce**ll phone.

4

Tricky Everyday Words

ACCIDENT

Miguel had an a**cc**ident: "The **c**ars **c**ollided, somehow, and now there's a dent... in the other car."

ACHIEVE

achieve

By the time Adam sat down to finish his glass of apple juice, **Eve** had already graduated from law school, designed her first intergalactic rocket and finished her speech in case she had to address the nation as a president. You see, **Eve** is an achi**eve**r and an unstoppable one too!

ADDRESS

address

"**Add** your **add**ress here," I was told before I **add**ed the **add**ress on the form.

ANSWER

"A very good answer will earn you **two ticks**," promised Miss Pell, as she set homework for next week.

ANXIETY

Andy suffers from e**x**am an**xie**ty. He is an**x**ious about a big **X** next to his answer.

"**An X i**n **e**xams is the worst that can happen!"

Trust yourself, Andy. You know more than you think you do.

APPEAR

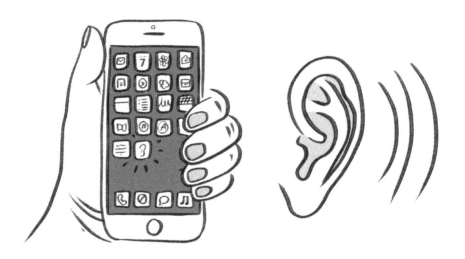

A new **app** has **app**eared to test your dominant **ear**.

You can now hold the phone to the right **ear**.

"Like this, Jorge. Get it right!"
"But what about people who hold it to the left **ear**?"

ARCHITECT

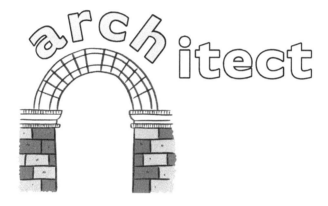

Is it true that only an **arch**itect can design an **arch**? My brother is an engineer.

Both **arch**itects and engineers design **arch**es. Engineers ensure **arch**es withstand strong physical pressure.

Architects make sure that **arch**es are pleasing to look at.

ARGUMENT

argument

Arnie's ar**gum**ent was that he could only think logically when he chewed **gum**: "No **gum**, no debate."

We couldn't argue with that.

AWKWARD

awkward
who
killed
who?

That a**wkw**ard moment when you watch a thriller with your buddies and have no idea **w**ho **k**illed **w**ho.

"Sorry to ask again: **W**HO **K**ILLED **W**HO?"

BARGAIN

bargain

"A good bar**gain** is always a **gain**," gasped Barney
before he rushed to the next shop.

BEAUTIFUL

be autiful
be   authentic

"To be **beau**tiful one has to **be au**thentic" is Adriana's life motto.

BEGINNING

In the beg**inni**ng, the world was created as a **mirror image** of the creator himself.

BELIEVE

believe

"I want to be**lie**ve him but what if it's a **lie**?" thought Lisa while packing her suitcase.

Michael had told her they were going on a vacation to Narnia.

BRAIN

brain

Bradley learned to spell "**bra**ke" after he avoided driving over a **bra**. The incident is still firmly stuck in his **bra**in.

Brain scans revealed **bra** images in the areas associated with a strong emotional response. The **bra** is actually in **Bra**dley's brain!

BRILLIANT

A br**illi**ant is a diamond with symmetrical edges that send sparkling beams of light. Br**illi**ant!

Now put that br**illi**ant away. The beams are making me **ill**.

BROCCOLI

broccoli
DOUBLE Vitamin C

Put **two C**s in *broccoli* because it contains MORE THAN **DOUBLE** vitamin **C** than lemons and limes.

While lemons and limes give us 31% of the Daily Value of Vitamin C, the figure goes up to 135% for bro**cc**oli.

CALENDAR

Only two months in the whole year start with an **A.**

Lend me a c**a**lend**a**r so I can check.

CARIBBEAN

Ca rib bean

Who would have thought that there is a **rib** and a **bean** in the dish associated with the Ca**ribbean** when spelling the word?

CASTLE

castle

Cast a spell, and a **cast**le appears!

CEMETERY

cemetery

Eeek!

Every time Celia had to pass through the c**em**e**te**ry, she was heard to utter a quiet "**Eee**k."

DEBT

Denis carried the **b**urden of his de**b**t with dignity.

DIFFERENT

Be diff**e**rent, **e**mbrace the change. Don't eliminate the **e** in the middle of the word. It gives you an **e**dge. It **e**mpowers you to do the things you've always wanted to do.

Emulate new **e**nergy to **e**mphasize your diff**e**rence.

EMBARRASS

When Fernando is emba**rr**a**ss**ed, he goes **r**eally **r**ed and **s**miles **s**hyly.

ENGINEER

Don't you sn**ee**r at an engin**ee**r.

They are hard-headed people, you know.

EQUIPMENT

When I said, "Get your equipment ready," I didn't mean your telephones.

There is no letter "t" in equipment, is there?

EXAGGERATE

exa **gg** erate

gentle
giant

My **ex**-boyfriend was a **g**entle **g**iant. People used to **exagg**erate that he was as big as a **g**reat **g**rizzly bear. To me, he was as small as a **g**rain of **g**old.
The only **gig**antic thing about my **g**entle **g**iant was his heart.

EXCELLENT

ex cellent
extra

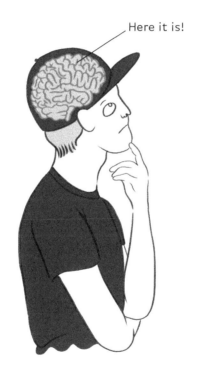

Here it is!

Why are some people **excell**ent problem solvers?

They must have an **ex**tra **cell** in their brains. How else would they come up with **excell**ent ideas like a three-day weekend?

FAMILIAR

familiar

"How can someone so fami**liar** be such a **liar**?" thought Gabriela looking at Isabel's boyfriend's nose. It seemed improbable that Isabel was not fami**liar** with the wooden puppet story.

"**Liar**, **liar**, pants on fire. Nose as long as a telephone wire..." sang Gabriela as she left the room.

FEBRUARY

Febr... uary

There is only one month in the whole year that makes me go "**Br**rr..."

Try standing on the freezing Brooklyn **Br**idge in Fe**br**uary.

FOREIGN

Euro is a for**e**ign currency.

The spelling of the word looks like it belongs to a "for**e**ign" language.

FORTUNATE

fortunate

Why is Pebbles the most for**tuna**te cat in the world?

He gets to eat lots of **tuna**.

Just check my **tuna**-exclusive cupboard. It's **for tuna** only.

FRIEND

friend

Frank wasn't simply a **Fri**day fri**end**.

He was a **friend** till the **end**!

GARAGE

What's that **rage** in the ga**rage**?

Rick bought a new car this morning.

It doesn't fit in the ga**rage**.

HICCUP

To cure a **hic**cup, try drinking from a **cup** while standing on your head.

HOMEOWNER

homeowner

Yes, "ho**meow**ner" is one word, I promise.

The cute sound effect in the middle of the word will help you remember who the real ho**meow**ner is!

Meow...

HONORABLE

hon or able

Are you **able** to act with **honor**? Whether **on or** off
duty? Do the right thing? Keep your promise?
Then you are a respect**able**, honor**able** person.
You have a spine.

IRRESISTIBLE

irresistible

My **sis**ter and **I** are irre**sis**tible.

By the way, I don't see any "table" in "irresistible,"
do you?

ISLAND

is land

Island is **land**.

If I could only take one thing to the desert **island**...

I wouldn't go.

ISSUE

Why **is Sue** the **issue** every time?

Possibly because she doesn't realize she **is** the **issue** every time.

JEALOUSY

jealousy

"Not many things in life make you feel as **lousy** as jea**lousy**," admitted **Jea**n's ex-boyfriend.

LEATHER

I eat her

"This l**eather** purse is so nice I could **eat her**!"
thought Lena while deciding whether to spend her last
$10 on lunch or accessories.

LEISURE

leisure
let's
eat
ice-cream

"**L**et's **e**at **i**ce-cream."

"**Sure**."

LIBRARY

library

Following his **bra**king incident to avoid driving over a **bra**, which left emotional and physical scars on his **bra**in, **Bra**dley decided to find self-help books in the li**bra**ry.

Little did he know that he would see another **bra** in the li**bra**ry.

MEDITERRANEAN

medi terra nean

never
eat
alone
Nico

Medi is the Latin root word for *middle*.

Terra is the Latin and Italian word for *land*.

Medi + **terra** = midland

Mediterranean = of middle land (between Europe and Africa) surrounded by water

nean = **n**ever **e**at **a**lone, **N**ico.

In the Mediterra**nean** culture, people have meals together. It is assumed to be one of the reasons why they live longer and enjoy better physical and mental health. Way to go, Nico!

MESSAGE

A Facebook **mess**age:

"My house isn't **mess**y. It's custom designed by my 3-year-old. We live in a new **mess age**, which gives children freedom to learn by exploring."

Like, comment, or share?

MONEY

Tell your friends (individually) they'll owe you **one** cent if you can read their mind.

Here's your script:

1. Pick a number between 1 and 10.
2. Multiply it by 9.
3. If you've got a 2-digit number, add the 2 digits together.
4. Take away 5.
5. Give your digit a letter: 1 = A, 2 = B, 3 = C, etc.
6. Think of a country that begins with that letter.
7. Now find the second letter in the country and think of an animal that begins with that letter.
8. Think of that animal's color.
9. Is it a gray elephant from Denmark?
10. Can I have one cent, please?

MUSCLE

muscle
clever

Mus**cle**s are **cle**ver. I'm not joking: they have memory, which is aptly called "mus**cle** memory."

When you practice a physical task over and over (think of bike riding, dancing, knitting, ball kicking or handwriting), it becomes easier and easier because your mus**cle**s seem to "remember" the action, or sequence of actions.

The interaction between your brain (memory systems) and your mus**cle**s (motor systems) results in this amazing efficiency. You know the rest: practice makes perfect.

PAVILION

pavilion

There might be very many **lion**s in a million, but there is only one **lion** in a pavi**lion**.

One lion, one "I".

PEOPLE

People live on Earth and the round planet (**O**) lives in the spelling of the word "pe**o**ple."

POSSESSES

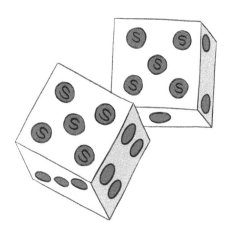

"Po**ss**e**ss**es" po**ss**e**ss**es **five S**s.

But what about

"po**ss**e**ss**ion," or

"po**ss**e**ss**ive"?

Four out of five is still impressive.

PRACTICE

practice

confidence

practice

Practice makes perfect, so go and practice confidence.

There's no "glory" in practice, only "**ice**." But without pract**ice**, there's no glory.

Practice till you get your **ice-c**old **c**onfidence. You **c**an do it!

PRAYER

Mom says that when a p**ray**er is said, a **ray** of sunshine appears in the sky.

Is that why she says a little p**ray**er every time she takes her laundry out to dry in the backyard?

RASPBERRY

raspberry
pick

"**P**ick me!" shouted the ras**p**berry.

Save distressed ras**p**berries from acting **p**eculiar—**p**ick them!

RECEIPT

You receive a recei**pt** for **p**ayment.

Promptly, I hope.

RECEIVE

When you **smile**, you r**ece**ive a smile back.

Public transport and hallways are great places to test this theory, but please don't stare or smile for longer than a couple of seconds.

Let me know how many smiles you r**ece**ived back.

RECOVER

recover

When my illness is **over**, I rec**over**.

Will I rec**over** what I paid (**over** the odds) for the vacation that made me sick? You bet.

RESTAURANT

"**Ey, you**! Get out of my rest**au**rant!" heard Carlos
after he'd tested food on nearby tables.
Not the wisest way to choose your dinner.

SAUSAGE

Although sa**usa**ges originated in Germany, the **U.S.A.** gave the world hotdogs and corndogs.

Mustard or ketchup with yours?

SCISSORS

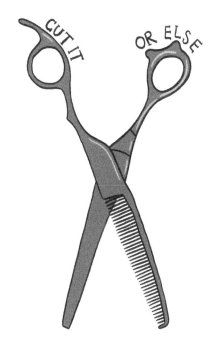

"**C**ut **i**t, **o**r **e**lse!" hissed a bald customer to his barber, who'd dropped his **sc**i**ss**o**r**s.

"Absolutely. I was just about to ask about your vacation," mumbled the barber, as he made a part in the customer's imaginary hair.

SEIZE

seize the day
simply existing is zero enjoyment

The phrase *carpe diem* means "**seize** the day." It was written by the Roman poet Horace, who believed we should enjoy our lives while we can.

"Everyone dies, but not everyone lives before they die," observed Mom looking in Dad's direction.

SPECIAL

Spencer was a spe**cia**l agent with the **CIA**.
He wore spe**cia**l glasses from spe**cia**list optometrists.

STAIRS

stairs

Alist**air** believed that running up and down the st**air**s gave his lungs more oxygen than jogging.

"More steps, more **air**!" he shouted before collapsing with a light head.

SURFACE

surf ace

On the **surface**, Al looked like an average person. One day, they felt a strong urge to be the best.

Fast forward to today, Al isn't just an **ace**, they are a **surf ace**!

TOGETHER

to get her

"To be **together**, I need **to get her**!" shouted Tommy.

Too late—Sandra disappeared around the corner.

TOMORROW

tom or row?

Brian could see **Tom or** go **row**ing **tomorrow**.

"**Tom or row**? Well, if the weather is good, I'll go rowing. If it's not good, I'll go rowing anyway."

TOUCH

touch

I told Tom that when I t**ouch** my neck, I can't help but scream "**Ouch**!" I had pulled a muscle.

Tom told me his story: "When we took Grandpa to a restaurant, we realized he's like a computer. We had to t**ouch** him every few minutes or he would fall asleep."

"**Ouch**! What?"

"It's okay, Grandpa. Thanks for letting me have your dessert."

Tom laughed but I wasn't t**ouch**ed by the story. I ate his snack to teach him a lesson. It was peanut butter and cucumber. **Ouch**...

VEGETABLE

We **get** healthy by eating ve**get**ables.

We also **get** more **able** (clever) at school.

Mom hates it when I don't eat my v**ege**tables: "Don't take them out and leave them on the **table**."

VICIOUS

vicious
vice

Committing crime is a **vic**e of **vic**ious people.

VILLAGE

Not all **villa**ges have a **villa** in them but those that do help us spell the word "**villa**ge."

WATCH

Watch out for the letter "**t**" in "wa**t**ch."

Not **T** for **T**imex but the silent "**t**" in the middle of the word "wa**t**ch."

WEDNESDAY

Wed nes day

"Payday is my favorite day."
"If I had a favorite day, it'd be **Wed-Nes-day**."
"You haven't even met **Nes**."
"I said, *if* I had a favorite day… I'd marry **Nes** any day."

"Even on a **Wednesday**?"

WEIRD

There is nothing strange, creepy or freaky about **we**ird creatures.

They are 100% a**we**some.

WRAP

"**W**rap it **w**ell or it will come undone," **w**arned **W**ilma at the exact time as **W**ill's beans, lettuce, tomatoes, mushrooms, corn and sweet chili sauce landed on her new **w**all-to-**w**all carpet.

YACHT

yacht
a
cruiser
heaven

Dad wants a y**ach**t: "Imagine **c**ruising the world in style. A y**ach**t is **a c**ruiser **h**eaven."

"More like bruiser **h**eaven." Mom reminds him of his recent RV accident, which left her leg in a cast for three weeks.

5

Academic and More Formal Words

ACCOMMODATE

"A**cc**o**mm**odate" is such a long word that it can accommodate not one, but **two C**s and **two M**s.

Ooh, a very nice window in your a**cc**o**mm**odation.

AMIABLE

am i able?

"**Am I able** to help you, Sir?"

"Oh, you're very **amiable**, Sir."

APPARENT

ap parent
app

Apparently, there is an **app** for **p**arents to control the amount of time kids spend on their electronic devices.

Unfortunately, the **app** requires the kids' help with **app**arent installation problems.

ASCERTAIN

as certain

When you **ascertain** (check) the facts, it makes you **as certain** as you can be.

ASSASSINATE

A **s**urprise **s**hot, then another **s**urprise **s**hot.

The target has been a**ss**a**ss**inated.

ATHEIST

a the ist
theory

An a**the**ist might want to disprove the existence of God or gods using **the**ory-based evidence.

BUREAUCRACY

bureaucracy

every admistrator using computers

"Why is there so much bur**eauc**racy these days?" lamented Mom.

"You've just switched jobs. What do you expect?" reminded Dad.

"I blame **e**very **a**dministrator **u**sing **c**omputers."

"Your new job *is* an administrator using computers, Sheila."

BUSINESS

bus in ess

essex

If it weren't for the good old **bus in Ess**ex, how would busy **business** people from the region get to their **business** meetings in London? The whole U.K. economy depends on the **bus in Ess**ex.

What's that, Buster? No good bu**sin**ess is free of **sin**?

CANDIDATE

candi date

Candi is going on a **date**.
She is very excited: "I hope he's a boyfriend **candidate**!"
If only she could see his planner. The **date** is written
on the wrong day!

CAPABILITY

cap ability

Hamza was especially able when he put his thinking **cap** on.

His outstanding cap**ability** was reported in local papers, which labeled him the "**cap-able**" boy.

CARICATURE

At which point do people become **caricat**ures of social media? When they take selfies in their **car**s, or selfies with their **cat**s.

"Give me Pebbles back, Mateo! And get out of my Porsche. **You're** a **caricat**ure of a man."

CHALLENGE

If it won't cha**lle**nge you, it won't **change** you.

Long-**l**asting **e**ffect guaranteed!

COMMITMENT

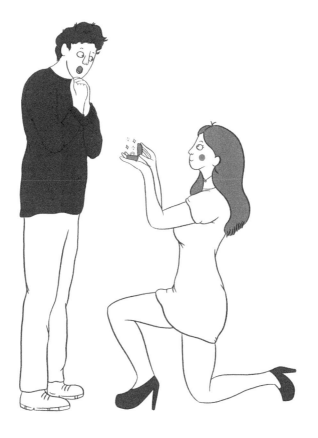

Mia expressed her co**mm**itment to Mark with two words: "**M**arry **m**e!"

CRITICIZE

criticize

Critics **critic**ize others by expressing unfavorable opinions about them.

Take Mom, the **cr**udest **critic** in the family: "Is it the dress that makes you look big, or...?"

"Mooom! Oh, forget it. I'm not going anywhere!"

"Why **critic**ize again, Sheila?" Dad always tries to be objective: "There is no 'size' in 'criti**cize**.' So don't **critic**ize people's size."

Think *criticize*, think *critic*.

Don't mention the size. Ever.

DEFINITE

def **in it** e

in it

I didn't know I'd be so lucky, but I was def**init**ely **in it** to win it!

DIARRHEA

diarrhea

**dash
in
a
real
rush
hurry
else
accident**

Nothing else to add here...

DILEMMA

Emma has a dil**emma**.
She gave her porcelain doll to G**emma**,
who dropped it when she felt a tremor.

G**emma** has now confided in J**emma**,
who thinks **Emma** should condemn her.
Is that how **Emma** should solve the dil**emma**?

DISCIPLINE

discipline

I **disc**ipline my dog by only letting him play with his **disc** when he's been good.

It's "**disc**-ipline."

ENVIRONMENT

Iron is in our env**iron**ment. Remember to put "**iron**" in the spelling too.

The United States recycles 85 million tons of **iron** and steel every year to save up the energy needed to make products from raw materials. That makes for a happy env**iron**ment!

FLUORESCENT

flu or e scent

Felix's eyes turned **flu**ore**scent**.
Was it because of his **flu**, **or E scent**s in the flu pills?

It's hard to tell but **E** numbers and flavored scents are best avoided.

FORESEEABLE

fore see able
front

Florence can **fore**see future events. You see, she is able to know what will happen in the near future.

Words that start with "**fore**" mean things that are at the front or close to us, for example "**fore**seeable" means "in the near future."

GIST

When you **get** the **gist** of something, you have a broad understanding of what has happened, or the text's key points.

Mind mapping is a great way to **get** the **gist**. **Get** it?

GLOSSARY

glossary

Without a g**loss**ary, I'm at a **loss**.

GOVERNMENT

gover nm ent
no money

A Politics exam question:

"The gover**nm**ent has **no** **m**oney of its own. It's all your money. Discuss."

GRAFFITI

gra ff iti
o ff ensive

"O**ff**ensive or not, gra**ff**iti is a form of art."

"Yes, but don't forget that gra**ff**iti is illegal."

"Right, I'm **off**!"

GRAMMAR

Poor gram**mar** doesn't reflect well on you.

What's that? The reflection in the mirror needs fixing? Why is "gram**mar**" always tricky?

Gramma Wilson won't know. She never had her "r" in the first place.

HERITAGE

heritage

Can we put a price **tag** on something as priceless as the national heri**tag**e?

HIERARCHY

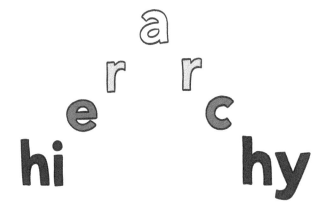

Dad showed me an uncanny **mirror image** chart that represents the order of social standing. Everyone seems to be above me!

Here's what it said:

A-list entries
Rank entries
Earn-your-**C**orn entries
And you: **Hi** there! **Hy**!

IMMEDIATELY

immediately
act

You need to do this immedi**a**tely.

Act now!

INDEPENDENT

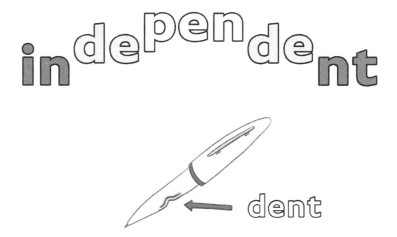

How do you tell if a journalist is inde**pendent**?

By a **dent** in their **pen**.

Another way to spell the word right is to picture **two** "**de**"s around "**pen**."

KNOWLEDGE

kn owl edge

Apparently, the **owl** has the most kn**owl**edge of all birds. No wonder the **owl** has the **edge**!

When I spell "knowl**edge**," I see an **owl** sitting on the **edge** of a branch.

Or I imagine the same **owl** feeling on **edge**!

LIAISON

lia i son

Liaison involves communicating with someone.

There was only one thing Tarzan wanted to communicate to **Lia**, his mom:

"**Lia, I son**."

LICENSE

license
sorry, officer

"**S**orry, officer. Here's my licen**s**e," Dad **s**miled **s**hyly.

"I'm afraid your licen**s**e has expired, Mr. Smith. You are not licen**s**ed to drive."

"Or **s**peed, if you ask me..." blurted out Mom.

"**S**orry, officer." Dad attempted another **s**hy **s**mile, then did a sharp head turn: "**S**hush! Or you'll be **s**orry, **S**heila!"

MANAGEMENT

management

Is your mana**gem**ent a **gem**? A shining example of an excellent company?

MANEUVER

man eu vre
elephants usually

Did you know that **e**lephants **u**sually man**eu**ver badly?

I've done an experiment so you don't have to.

You're welcome.

MEDIEVAL

medieval

People would **die** early in Me**die**val times. If it wasn't the Black Death, it was famine, violence or heresy.

If you know a handful of heretics in modern-day politics and media, you could say that old habits **die** hard.

MISCELLANEOUS

mis cell aneous

a
new
essay
on
U.S.

Catalina's lecturer set an assignment to research information for **a new essay on** the **U.S.** using **miscellaneous** (varied and diverse) sources, including articles, books, films, interviews and even music.

Catalina is currently in a nail salon two blocks away from the library.

"Didn't he say to look at different files?"

MISSPELL

Miss Pell

Miss Pell was a stickler for correct spelling.

"**Miss Pell**, I would never **misspell** a word to upset you," said Peter, self-proclaimed greatest fan of **Miss Pell**.

NOTICEABLE

notice able

before

after

"I hope you're **able** to **notice** the difference between the two boards. I worked really hard to make sure it's **noticeable**."

(>_<)

"Oh... You have **notice**d..."

OCCURRED

A déjà vu is when we have a feeling that our current experience has o**cc**u**rr**ed before.

There are **twice** the number of "**c**"s and "**r**"s in the spelling of "o**cc**u**rr**ed"—now check that each letter has o**cc**u**rr**ed **twice**.

OFFICIAL

official / official
office

The word "offi**cia**l," like "spe**cia**l," has links with the **CIA**. Have you seen the offi**cia**l **CIA** badge in real life? Me neither...

Worry not. If you ever forget how to spell **official**, you only need to think of **office**. The **Official Office for Tricky Spellings** springs to mind.

OPPORTUNITY

When an o**pp**ortunity knocks on your door, give **two** knocks back for a yes.

"If only Dad knew that," sighs Mom. "He knocks three times and wonders why nobody answers."

PARALLEL

Not many things are as parallel as train tracks.

The tracks in the spelling literally show the meaning of "parallel."

PARLIAMENT

parl i am ent

How do you become a parl**iam**ent? You "forget" to summon it, as Charles I did in 17th century Britain. For 11 years, he *was* the parl**iam**ent!

Ah, I almost forgot—that didn't work out very well. He was later beheaded for treason...

PERSISTENT

persis tent

No one is more per**sis**tent than my **sis**ter. She should hold the world record for taking the slowest time to put up a **tent**.

"To be per**sistent** is to refuse to quit," says my **sis**. "If I stopped trying to put up the **tent**, where would I sleep tonight?"

PHARAOH

ph ara oh

My history teacher joked that Ancient Egypt wouldn't have fallen to the Roman Empire if the ph**araoh**s had succeeded in teaching their **ara**s to repeat the emperors' secret conversations.

"**Oh**" was the most they achieved.

PHYSICIAN

phy sic ian
sick

It's easy to confuse phy**sic**ians with physicists. Phy**sic**ians treat **sic**k people, and physicists research physics.

Take **Ian**. He became a phy**sic**ian to heal the **sic**k.

PRECISE

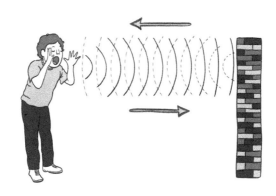

What is never wrong?
Echo.
It can compete with recording apps for word-for-word pr**ecis**ion.

Pr**ecise** means: **e**xactly **c**orrect, **in s**hort: **e**cho.

PREJUDICE

"It's silly to be mean to someone just because they have different colored spots," concluded 4-year-old **Judi** after her mom used **dice** to explain the word "pre**judice**."

PRIVILEGE

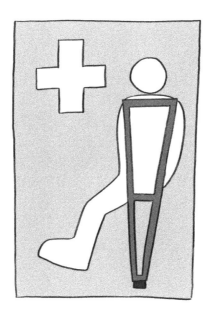

A broken **leg**? It's your privi**leg**e to use a special seat.

PROFESSOR

| One F | **one f**ace | check | ✓ |
| Two Ss | **two s**pecs | check | ✓ |

What is the pro**fess**or still looking for?

PROPAGANDA

propaganda

Is Halloween a pro-**pagan** celebration?

Sofia seems to think so: "The only thing we learn from Halloween is that pretending to be someone else, not working hard and living a good life, results in a sweet reward."

PUBLICLY

To be truly effective when speaking public**ly**, you need to **l**ove **y**ourself. Thanks, Justin.

If you thought public speaking was your ally, think again—there is no -ally at the end of the word. Only -**ly**, **l**ove **y**ourself.

QUESTIONNAIRE

questionnaire

no
answer
is
right
eddie

"I'm afraid **n**o **a**nswer **is r**ight, **E**ddie."

"But it's a question**naire**, not a test!"

RECOMMEND

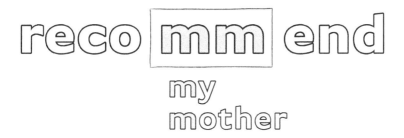

Any job anywhere: big, small, in house, out of house, skilled, semi-skilled, tough, late hours—I reco**mm**end **m**y **m**om!

RESEARCH

research

When I think of re**sea**rch, I first imagine a **sea** of papers. Books, articles, printouts, slides, notes, sticky notes—a dangerous, cold and unforgiving **sea**.

But if you tread carefully, the same **sea** can be awe-inspiring, breathtaking, mesmerizing and actually rather beautiful.

RESOURCE

resource

Human Resources

Some meetings to discuss re**sour**ces are more "**sour**" than others.

RHYTHM

rhythm

rhythm
has
your
two
hips
moving

"I want to take Zhuang to the prom," announced my sister. "But what if he has no **rhythm**?"
"Surely he has heartbeat. Unless your news was too much for him! Wait... Hadn't he given his heart away before you asked?"
"Very funny, Miss Jealous."

SCHEDULE

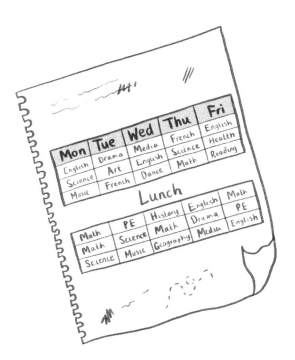

Bus **sch**edule, mail delivery **sch**edule, work **sch**edule, house chore **sch**edule?

Think *school schedule* to remember the spelling of any **sch**edule.

SEPARATE

sep a rat e

Sep**arat**e the sheep from the goats and remember to leave **a rat** in "sep**arat**e."

SIGNIFICANT

sign if i cant

"Please **sign** here."
"What **if I can't**?"
"Then we've got a **significant** problem. No **sign**ature, no loan."

SLAUGHTER

slaughter

Stop laughing and put the chicken down, you beast! **Slaughter** is never **laughter** (unless you think of the word's spelling).

SUCCESS

If, at first, su**cc**e**ss** avoids you, you and I have a lot in common. Unless your road to su**cc**e**ss** is always under construction, in which case I suggest you deactivate your TikTok, Snapchat and Instagram accounts.

SUCCINCT

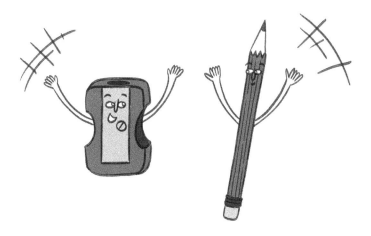

What did the pencil sharpener say to the pencil? Stop going in circles and get to the point!

For speech or writing to be su**cc**inct, it has to be brief, clearly expressed and to the point: **c**ompact and **c**lear.

THESAURUS

the sau Я us
speedy
assignment
upgrade

Ted has discovered a the**sau**rus: "I feel like I'm in a **toy shop**! So many words to choose from. A **s**peedy **a**ssignment **u**pgrade every time."

VACUUM

A Philosophy exam question:

"How soon do you become a vac**uum** cleaner when you clean a vac**uum** cleaner?"

VEHICLE

vehicle

What do you call a car with a **hic**cup?

A ve**hic**le.

VILLAIN

villa in

"**Villa in** you live?" asked Yoda.
"I do, do I?" answered the **villa**in.
"Live not on evil," replied Yoda in the **villa**in's
speaking style.

6

Copyright Note

Many mnemonics used in this book are in public domain—they are widely used by teachers, parents and grandparents. They are shared and handed down from one generation to another. Stylistic variations exist but the underlying ideas have remained unchanged for years. For this reason, it's virtually impossible to trace the exact origin of a particular mnemonic.

Around half of the spelling hints in this book have been collected over the past 15 years when the author worked as a dyslexia support tutor, study skills tutor and psychology teacher. Very many enthusiastic students have shared their favorite mnemonics with her.

The other half are spelling hints created by the author and her students, in particular college teacher training students preparing for their national spelling tests. These mnemonics had to pass their tough test of effectiveness before appearing in this book.

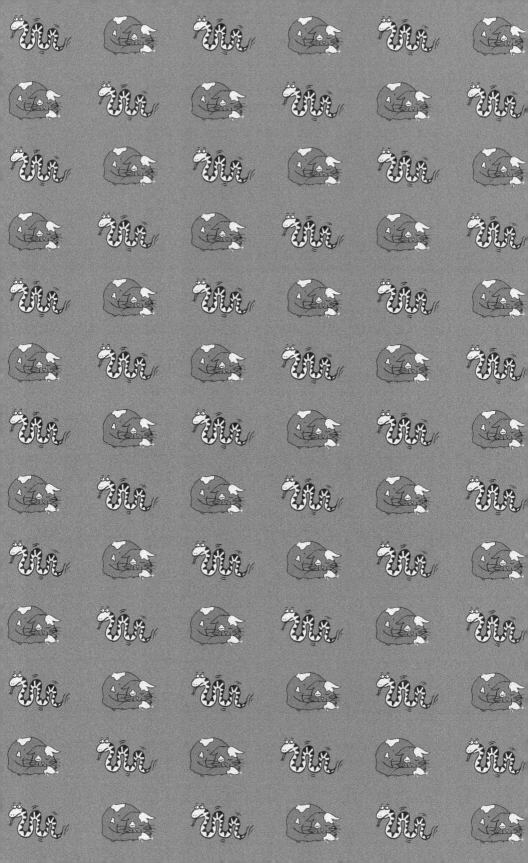

7

References

Architect

Margolius, I. (2008) *Architects + Engineers = Structures*. Cambridge, MA: Academic Press.

Bear

Bedolfe, S. (2012) *The School: Polar Bear Adaptations for Extreme Cold. One World One Ocean Campaign.* Available at: www.oneworldoneocean.com/%20blog/entry/the-school-polar-bear-adaptations-for-extreme-cold, accessed on 09 June 2020.

Bored

Crow, S. (2018) You'll Spend This Much of Your Life Waiting at Red Lights. *Bestlife*. Available at: https://bestlifeonline.com/red-lights, accessed on 09 June 2020.

Broccoli

The World's Healthiest Foods (2020) *Vitamin C*. Available at: www.whfoods.com/genpage.php?tname=nutrient&dbid=109, accessed on 09 June 2020.

Chile

Kids World Travel Guide (2020) *Chile Facts: Chile Geo Superlatives.* Available at: www.kids-world-travel-guide.com/chile-facts.html, accessed on 09 June 2020.

McCarthy, C., Raub, K., St Louis, R., Brown, C. and Johanson, M. (2018) *Lonely Planet Chile & Easter Island (Travel Guide).* Franklin, TN: Lonely Planet.

College

The Big Bang Theory (2007) Directed by Mark Cendrowski. CBS series. DVD.

Desert

Parker, S. (2009) *Deserts (Planet Earth).* London: QED Publishing.

Dessert

Durand, M. (2013) *French Words, Phrases and Sentences 1000+*. US: CreateSpace Independent Publishing Platform.

Environment

Business Recycling (2016) *Why Recycle?* Available at: https://businessrecycling.com.au/recycle/iron-steel, accessed on 09 June 2020.

West, L. (2019) The Benefits of Metal Recycling. *Thought Co.* Available at: www.thoughtco.com/the-benefits-of-metal-recycling-1204149, accessed on 09 June 2020.

Flower

Thompson, I. (2013) *Summer of '67: Flower Power, Race Riots, Vietnam and the Greatest Soccer Final Played on American Soil.* US: CreateSpace Independent Publishing Platform.

Government

Aitken, J. (2013) *Margaret Thatcher: Power and Authority*. London: Bloomsbury Continuum Publishing.

Isle

East London History (2014) *History of The Isle of Dogs London*. Available at: www.eastlondonhistory.co.uk/isle-of-dogs-london, accessed on 09 June 2020.

Lose

Cooper, B.B. (2013) 8 Subconscious Mistakes Our Brains Make Every Day - And How to Avoid Them. *Fast Company*. Available at: www.fastcompany.com/3019903/8-subconscious-mistakes-our-brains-make-every-day-and-how-to-avoid-them, accessed on 09 June 2020.

Mediterranean

Online Etymology Dictionary (2020) *Mediterranean*. Available at: www.etymonline.com/word/mediterranean, accessed on 09 June 2020.

Mnemonic

Finding Nemo (2003) Directed by Andrew Stanton. Pixar Animation Studios. DVD.

Muscle

Darebee (2020) *Muscle Memory Explained*. Available at: https://darebee.com/fitness/muscle-memory-explained.html

Money

FC (2016) Grey Elephant in Denmark. *Finance in the Classroom Educational Re-sources* (downloads). Available at: http://financeintheclassroom.org, accessed on 09 June 2020.

Parliament

Scarboro, D. (2005) England 1625–1660: Charles I, The Civil War and Cromwell. *SHP Advanced History Core Texts.* London: Hodder Education.

President

History (2020) *U.S. Presidents*. Available at: www.history.com/topics/us-presidents, accessed on 09 June 2020.

Their

O'Brien, C. (2016) *The Little Book of Irish Jokes*. Chichester: Summersdale Publishers.

Wear

Sherrow, V. (2001) *For Appearances' Sake: The Historical Encyclopedia of Good Looks, Beauty, and Grooming.* Portsmouth: Greenwood Publishing Group.

Index